EDITH CAVELL

The story of a Norfolk nurse

Sheila Upjohn

Front Page photograph
Edith Cavell's memorial statue
beside the Erpingham Gate to Norwich Cathedral Close

Edith Cavell

The story of a Norfolk nurse

First published in Great Britain 2000
Norwich Cathedral Publications Ltd
12 The Close
Norwich
NR1 4DH

ISBN 0 9535493 3 x

All profits from the sale of this book are covenanted to:
The Friends of Norwich Cathedral

Printed in Great Britain by
Catton Print, Norwich.

Contents

ACKNOWLEDGEMENTS vi

FOREWORD BY CANON PHILLIP McFADYEN vii

Growing Up 1

Leaving Home 5

Nursing as a Vocation 7

Nursing Abroad 11

War Breaks Out 16

The Resistance 19

Imprisonment 23

The Trial 25

Edith's Final Hours 28

The World Reads 33

Recommended for further reading 43

ACKNOWLEDGEMENTS

Front cover photograph by courtesy of the Eastern Daily Press, Norwich.

Black and white photographs by kind permission of
The Royal London Hospital.

Colour photographs by Martin Miller.

The Dean & Chapter Library, Norwich Cathedral.

FOREWORD

There are two great statues in the environs of Trafalgar Square, both dedicated to the memory of Norfolk heroes – Nelson and Edith Cavell. What is not often realised is that both of them were raised in Norfolk Vicarages.

When I was Vicar of Swardeston, I used to impress this knowledge on our children in the hope that it would encourage them. Life in a Vicarage can be 'trying' as Edith once wrote to her cousin Eddie Cavell. We all need to expand our horizons. Reading how others have done so often helps.

This little biography of Edith Cavell shows us how an ordinary Norfolk girl could capture the imagination of the world by being herself. The jingoism of the time wanted to portray her as an icon of martyrdom and it is true that recruitment to the first world war effort jumped considerably when news of her execution was released. She, however, saw herself as a 'nurse who simply did her duty'. She understood her duty to be ready to assist those in need and when necessary to convey them to safety. She was ready to get involved even at the risk of arrest. Her readiness to help, her simple faith in God and her unassuming humility is certainly worth revisiting. Norwich Cathedral Publications are proud to publish the story of one who reminds us that patriotism is not enough. Parochialism needs its horizons expanding. Edith Cavell and Lord Nelson are great examples of how to put this into practice.

Canon Phillip McFadyen
RANWORTH VICARAGE
FORMER VICAR OF SWARDESTON

Swardeston Church, Norfolk

Growing Up

Memories fade with years and, as the 100th anniversary of Edith Cavell's death approaches, people may start to wonder why the statue of this Norfolk nurse stands beside the West gate of Norwich cathedral and why she is buried beside its walls.

The story begins in 1865 when a baby girl, their first child, was born to the Reverend Frederick Cavell and his wife Louisa at the village of Swardeston five miles outside Norwich. They called her Edith. Fifty years later her name was to echo round the world.

Edith Cavell's life began conventionally enough. Two more girls and a boy were born to the Cavells and they grew up in the spacious new vicarage at Swardeston, which their father built at his own expense. It cost £1,500 – a sum that all but ruined him.

Swardeston Vicarage, where Edith grew up.
Her parents continued to live here until her father
retired in 1909, just before his 85th birthday.

Edith's father taught her at home until she was 16
– about the age this photograph was taken.
She then went to three different boarding schools.

There was no school in the village until Edith was five, but the vicarage girls did not go to school with the village children – their father taught them at home. Then in 1881, when Edith was 16, her father decided to send her to the Norwich High School in Theatre Street for a few months. She used to walk the five miles from Swardeston, dropping off her eight year-old brother at Miss Brewer's school in Lime Tree Road on the way. The Cavells did not own a pony and trap (perhaps because the house had proved so costly), there were no cars, and the chain-driven bicycle, which soon drove the pennyfarthing off the market, was not invented until Edith was 20. So Edith and her brother were used to walking long distances – like most people in those days.

After the High School, Frederick Cavell decided it was time to send his daughter to a boarding school – probably regarding it as an opportunity for her to broaden her experience of life. He himself had sent his own wife to a finishing school before they were married. She was the daughter of his housekeeper, who was "a widowed gentlewoman in reduced circumstances" and so had not had the opportunity for the education he thought necessary for a vicar's wife.

So between the ages of 16 and 19 Edith was sent to three different boarding schools – in London, in Bristol and in Peterborough. At the last school, Laurel Court, she was a pupil-teacher. Haphazard though this schooling seems to have been, one thing was to stand Edith in good stead. Laurel Court excelled in languages and many of the girls came from France, Germany, Holland and Denmark. Edith became fluent in French. Five years later she was to take a post in Brussels on the recommendation of her old headmistress Miss Gibson – a decision that was to change her life.

After her time at Laurel Court the 19 year-old Edith went home to Swardeston to be the vicar's dutiful daughter. She taught at the Sunday School, went visiting with her mother, played the new game of lawn tennis and made watercolour sketches. But she did something more than that. Realising that her father badly needed a Church Room to house the growing Sunday School, she took it upon herself to write to the Bishop of

Norwich about it. Bishop Pelham agreed to help, providing the village itself raised some of the money. So Edith and her sister Florence set to work, painting watercolours, drawing sketches and making Christmas cards – all of which they sold. Within a year they had raised £300 – and the Sunday School was built.

The church at Swardeston was the centre of Edith Cavell's early life. She taught in the Sunday school and she and her sister helped raise the money to build the new Sunday school room.

Leaving Home

That autumn Edith left home and took a post as governess in another clergy family at Steeple Bumpstead in Essex. There were three girls, aged 11, 9 and 8, and a little boy of 6. Edith taught them all subjects, including French and music, and was also responsible for their clothes and their free-time activities. On top of this, the vicar's wife was an invalid and Edith had to undertake many of her duties, including organising bazaars, arranging church flowers and acting as hostess. In summer she took charge of the children for a month's holiday at Clacton.

Edith stayed three years, until the parents decided the children were too old for a governess. Back home in Swardeston she went as governess to the children of the Gurneys at Keswick Hall and the Barclays at Colney Hall, working three days a week for each. After that she took a post with the Pryor family at Chelmsford.

Very few professions were open to women in the 1880s and the 19 year-old Edith's first job was as a governess to the children of another clergy family.

After a year came the opportunity of working abroad. A wealthy Brussels family asked her old headmistress at Laurel Court to recommend an English governess who spoke fluent French, and Miss Gibson put Edith Cavell's name forward. The family lived in one of the most fashionable streets in Brussels. There were four children – Marguerite 13, Georges 12, Helene 8 and Eveline 3. There followed five happy years.

But in 1895 something happened that was to end Edith's career as a governess. Her father fell ill and she came home to nurse him. By the end of the year she knew she had found her vocation. In December, a few days after her thirtieth birthday, she became an assistant nurse at *The Fountains Fever Hospital* in Tooting. Four months later, in April 1896, she was accepted for training at *The London Hospital*.

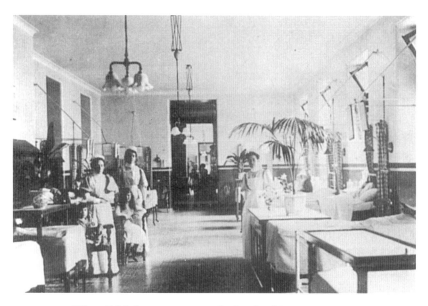

When Edith began to train at the London Hospital in 1896
the wards were heated by coal fires and lit by gas lamps.

Nursing as a Vocation

Nursing had only recently become a profession a respectable woman could enter. When Florence Nightingale had announced her intention of nursing, her mother and sister had collapsed in hysterics – and small wonder. "It was *preferred*," wrote Florence Nightingale in 1854, "that nurses should be women who had lost their characters." (i.e. had at least one illegitimate child). Discipline and supervision were almost non-existent, and a physician at a leading London hospital reported: "The nurses are all drunkards, Sisters and all, and there are but two nurses whom the surgeons can trust to give the patients their medicine." It was not uncommon for nurses to be part-time prostitutes.

Things had changed for the better when Edith Cavell began to nurse – thanks largely to the work of *The Nightingale Training School* which had opened just thirty five years earlier. Perhaps because of the bad name nursing had once carried, discipline was strict. The day began with the rising bell at 6am, breakfast was at 6.30am, and ward duty at 7am. Nurses did not come off duty until 9 o'clock at night, having been allowed half an hour for midday dinner and two hours off duty during the day. Supper was 9.20pm and Lights Out at 10pm. Lectures had to be attended in off duty hours, and nurses who had been on night duty had to get up to attend them. Probationers had one day off a fortnight and two weeks holiday a year.

Their off duty hours were strictly supervised. Nurses were forbidden to go out with doctors or medical students. The hospital porters were expected to keep watch and report to the Matron cases of nursing staff meeting doctors and students after hours. The penalty – for the nurse – was instant dismissal.

Pleasures were simple. Since a probationer's salary was £12 – not a week, or a month, but a year – they had to be. One of Edith Cavell's contemporaries at *The London* wrote: "During our leisure hours, weather permitting, we would ride on the top of a bus from the hospital to the Bank of England and back, our bonnets and cloaks were very familiar to

*Outside the London Hospital the children played on the streets
and the horse buses had made their appearance. Edith and her
fellow nurses used to make the trip to the Bank of England and
back for the fare of 1 penny.*

*Edith Cavell wrote to tell the matron of the
London Hospital, Eva Luckes, that she
had been appointed Assistant Matron of
the Shoreditch Infirmary.*

*Edith in the uniform of Assistant Matron of the Shoreditch Infirmary.
She was responsible for the day-to-day running of the wards and
teaching of the probationers.*

the bus drivers and conductors who frequently refused to accept our fare of one penny… Occasionally, on a Saturday, we were allowed to go in a beautiful launch down the river to Tilbury with a lovely basket of cakes, sandwiches and tea provided by one of our wealthy governors."

Edith stayed at *The London* for just over four years, including a three-month spell at Maidstone during which half a dozen nurses from *The London* were sent to nurse victims of the typhoid epidemic raging in the town. She also spent a year nursing private patients in their own homes. But, surprisingly, she was never made a Sister, and eventually she decided it was time to move to another hospital.

Her next post was Night Superintendent at *The St Pancras Infirmary*, a hospital which – like *The London* – was surrounded by slums. Most of the patients were not just ill, but desperately poor and undernourished. After three years she left to become Assistant Matron at *Shoreditch Infirmary* – another hospital in a very poor area. Here part of her job was to teach the probationers – something she found very rewarding.

Then, in March 1906 she wrote to Miss Luckes, her old Matron at *The London*:

"I have now been nursing for ten consecutive years without a break and feel very much in need of a long rest. The chance has come through the proposal of a friend that I should accompany her to the South of England and possibly abroad for three months. I am very anxious to accept but fear it would be difficult to find another suitable post… Would you very kindly help me in August, when I should be ready to return to work, if I wrote to you then?"

Back from her holiday Edith returned to Swardeston. It was not until March the following year that she managed to find another job – a temporary post as a Queen's District Nurse in Manchester. She was now 41 and still had not been given the responsibility she so plainly deserved. Then, in June 1907, came the opportunity she had been waiting for.

Nursing Abroad

In England, Florence Nightingale's energy and determination had transformed the nursing profession, but in Belgium there was still no training school for nurses and a Brussels physician, Dr Antoine Depage, determined to set one up. He wanted as Matron an Englishwoman who spoke fluent French and who had been trained at one of the famous London hospitals. Edith Cavell fitted the bill perfectly. And she had a further recommendation. Her name was already well known to the president of the Ladies Committee of the new nursing school, her son had married Marguerite Francois – the girl who had been Edith's pupil in Brussels all those years before.

The Francois children became firm friends with Edith when she was their governess. Here Marguerite holds Edith's hand, while her brother proudly displays his new bicycle.

When Edith reached Brussels she found the work to be accomplished was formidable. First, there were the premises to be prepared. Dr Depage had acquired four adjoining houses almost opposite his practice, and it was her job to turn these into a first-class teaching hospital. When she arrived little had been done. She wrote to her former Matron at *The London* on September 19th 1907:

"I arrived four days ago and found the four houses only partly furnished and in much confusion, and the Committee absent on holiday... no servants, only a portress, and nothing furnished but my sitting room – and we have to open on October 1st."

And as well as practical problems, there were prejudices to be overcome. Nursing was not thought to be a respectable occupation for a gentle-woman and most Belgian nurses were nuns who, though compassionate, had received no training. So middle-class families were reluctant to send their daughters to the new school, while the religious authorities were suspicious that this new venture would undermine their authority. Edith Cavell opened the "clinique" with just four probationary nurses.

The premises of the new training school in Brussels consisted of four adjoining houses. There were no interconnecting doors. Patients had to be carried down the stairs of one house, out into the street, and up the stairs of the adjoining house.

At first there was little equipment. Water had to be boiled in saucepans for sterilising. There were no lifts. Patients had to be carried down the stairs of one house, out into the street, and up the stairs of the adjoining house. "We were more like a family than anything else," Edith Cavell wrote. Little by little the enterprise gained momentum and respectability. The breakthrough came when the Queen of the Belgians broke her arm and sent to the new school for a trained nurse. Its status was assured.

Edith designed the uniform for her young nurses, as well as supervising their training. "We were more like a family than anything else", she wrote.

*The house in College Road, Norwich, which Edith's father had built
for his retirement. It was here that the news of Edith's death was
brought to her mother in 1915.*

Soon it was attracting trainee nurses from all over Europe. English, French, German, Swiss, Russian, Greek and Dutch girls – as well as Belgians – enrolled at the school. Edith Cavell looked after every detail, even designing their uniform. She wrote:

"They wear blue cotton dresses with high white aprons, white linen sleeves to cover the forearm, which is bare beneath. Their caps are of the plain Sister Dora type, without strings and without collars. The contrast they present to the nuns in their heavy stiff robes and the lay nurses with their grimy apparel is the contrast of the unhygienic past with the enlightened present."

Within five years nursing in Belgium was transformed. A new hospital, staffed by Cavell-trained nurses, was opened at St Gilles. Soon the training school was outgrowing its premises, and plans were made for a new teaching hospital to replace it. Dr Depage reported:

"The Belgian school of nursing has been an entire success… it now provides the nurses for three hospitals, three private nursing homes, twenty four communal schools and thirteen kindergartens in Brussels."

Edith's father died in 1910, aged 85, only a year after retiring from Swardeston. Her mother tried the experiment of living in Brussels – but could not get used to foreign ways. She was far happier back home in Norwich at 24 College Road, the house her husband had had built for their retirement. Edith wrote to her regularly, and every summer came back to England to spend her summer holiday at the little fishing village of West Runton on the north Norfolk coast. Her mother often joined her there. And it was during one of these Norfolk holidays in 1914 that an urgent telegram reached her from Brussels. War with Germany was imminent.

War Breaks Out

Edith went straight back to Belgium. Her first task was to prepare the clinic to receive the wounded, then to hang out Red Cross flags all over the house. The German invasion was not long in coming. Nineteen days after war was declared, German troops marched into Brussels. Edith Cavell wrote in The *Nursing Times:*

"In the afternoon [August 20] with much pomp and circumstance of war, the German troops marched into Brussels, and to the Town Hall, where the brave tricolour came down and the German stripes of black and white and red took its place... The troops were all in grey, with their brass helmets covered and their arms of dull steel. There are at least 20,000 who entered the city that day and camped in it for the night... On August 21 many more troops came through; from our road we could see the long procession, and when the halt was called at mid-day and carts came up with supplies, some were too weary to eat and slept on the pavement of the street... Some of the Belgians spoke to the invaders in German, and found they were very vague as to their whereabouts, and imagined they were already in Paris; they were surprised to be speaking to Belgians and could not understand what quarrel they had with them... I am but a looker-on, after all, for it is not my country whose soil is being desecrated, and whose sacred places are laid waste. I can only feel the deep and tender pity of a friend within the gates, and observe with sympathy and admiration the high courage and self control of a people enduring a long terrible agony. They have grown thin and silent with the strain. They walk about the city shoulder to shoulder with the foe and never see them, or make a sign; only they leave the cafes which they frequent, and turn their backs to them, and live a long way off and apart."

A few days later an event occurred that was to change Edith Cavell from a looker-on into an active participant in the war. Just thirty miles away from Brussels – near enough for Edith and her nurses to hear the guns – the British Expeditionary Force was defeated by the German Army at the Battle of Mons. "There has been terrible loss of life on both sides," Edith wrote. "We are doing no work among the wounded as everything is taken out of our hands at present and the enemy have made their own arrangements…. We are busy making garments for the poor, there will be great need of them this winter – there are so many refugees and so many homeless."

Two months later three men arrived at the clinic. They asked to see Edith Cavell. The spokesman was Herman Capiau, a mining engineer. With him, wounded and in disguise, were two British soldiers – Colonel Dudley Boger who had commanded the Cheshires at Mons and Sergeant Meachin. Both had been captured, but had managed to escape. Herman Capiau explained that the two men had been on the run for weeks and needed to stay in a safe house in Brussels until they could be smuggled out of the country. Would Miss Cavell help?

Colonel Dudley Boger, Edith Cavell's first "guest". When she saw his wounds she took him in without hesitation.

Edith Cavell looked at their wounds. Colonel Boger's foot was in a terrible state. The sock had eaten into the wound, which was in danger of turning gangrenous. Sergeant Meachin had a scalp wound. Her response was decisive. Dismissing Capiau, she took the men to adjoining rooms in her own part of the clinic, dressed their wounds and gave them a meal. They stayed for two weeks. Afterwards she wrote guardedly to her mother: "We have had some interesting work, but are now quiet again. Our people who left last week must have arrived safely, as they have not returned." From now on she was in the Resistance movement up to her neck.

German troops pose in front of the Town Hall in Brussels, where Edith saw them haul down the Belgian tricolour and raise the German flag on August 20th, 1914.

The Resistance

The escape network was a mixed collection of people, brought together by their determination to defy the invading Germans. It included the Prince and Princess de Croy – whose castle was not far from the battlefield at Mons – a school mistress, a barrister, a miner's wife, a chemist, a seamstress, an engineer, a market stall holder, the Comtesse de Belleville, a miner, an inn-keeper, an architect – and many more, all drawn together in their efforts to shelter soldiers cut off from their regiments and to smuggle them over the border into neutral Holland.

After her first two visitors Edith Cavell sheltered a stream of soldiers in the clinic – some British and some French. Then, two days before Christmas, Sergeant Jesse Tunmore of the Norfolk Regiment arrived, having found his own way to the clinic. Edith asked him how she could be sure he was a British soldier. He pointed to the picture of Norwich Cathedral on her office wall. "That's Norwich Cathedral," he said. "You know Norwich, do you?" said Edith Cavell. "Well, I know Norwich, too." He and several other British soldiers spent that Christmas hidden in the cellars of the clinic. Edith Cavell served them roast beef, and Christmas pudding made to her mother's recipe.

When an escaping prisoner arrived unescorted, Edith feared he might be a spy. "That's Norwich Cathedral," he said, pointing to a picture on her wall. Edith put her arms around him. "I'd do anything to help a Norfolk man", she replied.

On Christmas Day she gave a party to local children to which she also invited the Reverend Stirling Gahan, the only British clergyman still in Brussels. He later wrote: "I joined the party in the late hours of the afternoon and found a good many friends there… Nurse Cavell moved pleasantly among her guests and there, to our great amusement and delight, were a couple of British 'tommies'. How we gripped hands!"

Sergeant Tunmore eventually succeeded in getting back to Norwich. He wrote to Edith's mother: "I am writing to you to say that your daughter, the Matron of the Nurses' School in Brussels, is quite well. I am a soldier of the 1st Norfolks and she has done a lot for me in helping me to escape over the frontier to Holland."

For nine months Edith Cavell gave shelter to escaping soldiers. On one occasion she had to whisk one of them into bed, still wearing his army boots, when the Germans made a routine inspection. Once, when the Germans made a surprise raid at midnight, she was just in time to rouse a badly wounded soldier, help him into a barrel in an outhouse, and hide him by tipping apples over him. The Germans clanked through the yard and found nothing.

At one time there were as many as thirty five soldiers in the clinic. Some stayed a night or two, others for weeks. Edith Cavell did her best to keep all this a secret from her nurses, so they would not be implicated. As numbers increased, soldiers were hidden in the attic. Edith Cavell allowed them to go out in the evening, provided they kept to the quiet streets in groups of no more than two. One night half a dozen Irishmen met up in one of the local cafés, got drunk, and clattered back to the clinic singing "It's a long way to Tipperary" at the top of their voices – this in a street where German officers were billeted. They were promptly locked in and whisked off to other safe houses next day.

As well as nursing and feeding the soldiers, Edith Cavell photographed them for false passports, provided them with clothes and money, and often acted as their guide to rendezvous points in Brussels.

One of the men she saved was Private Robert Mapes of the 1st Norfolks, who had a bullet wound through his ankle. When she heard the way he spoke, Edith Cavell asked where he came from. "I'm from Hethersett, ma'am," he replied. "I know it well. It's near Swardeston where I was born," she said. Then she put her arms round him and kissed him. "Dear old Norfolk. I'd do anything to help a Norfolk man."

Private Robert Mapes, a soldier of the Norfolk Regiment whom Edith sheltered, came from Hethersett. When he got home he found his name on the Roll of Honour for the dead in Hethersett church.

But by the end of June the danger of discovery was becoming so great that Princess Marie de Croy called at the clinic to say the escape operation must stop. Edith Cavell was relieved. The day before she had been just in time to burn documents about soldiers before the Germans searched her office. Then she asked: "Are there any more hidden men?" The Princess told her that over thirty more had just been found in Cambrai. "Then we cannot stop," said Edith, "because if a single one of these men were taken and shot, that would be our fault."

During July there were more German inspections, and several bogus refugees who did not know the password (which was Yorc – Croy backwards) arrived asking for shelter and were turned away. But the mission went on. Among the last soldiers Edith Cavell helped escape were two men from the Irish Rifles. She disguised them as white-robed monks – a silent order – and saw them on to a tram. In spite of wearing army boots, they got through successfully.

Conscious that every day brought greater danger, and determined not to destroy more papers, Edith Cavell took precious documents to a nearby café where the owner let her hide them under a loose floorboard. But time was running out. On 31st July 1915, Phillipe Baucq – an architect who had helped mastermind the escape organisation – and Louise Thuliez – a school teacher who was another key figure – were arrested. Five days later the German Secret Police came for Edith Cavell.

Imprisonment

She was taken first to Police Headquarters and then to St Gilles prison. Questioning began three days later. Her interrogators were kind and courteous. Their technique was simple. They named all the other 34 members of the escape organisation who had been arrested and told her each had made a detailed confession of the details of the operation. Any denial or refusal to corroborate their evidence could result in harsher sentences for all the prisoners.

Edith Cavell believed them. All her life she had been surrounded by people of integrity and she herself was meticulously honest. As a young governess in Brussels she had even refused to say that Mme Francois was "not at home" to callers if, in fact, she was in the house. During repeated questioning over the next three weeks she made a detailed confession.

Here, too, she trusted the men who were interviewing her. She spoke in French with her interrogators, but her replies were written down in German. The statements she had made were then read back to her in French, but the actual document she signed was written in German – so she could not check its accuracy. She was therefore at the mercy of the translator. Part of her second statement made on 18th August reads: "I stress the fact that, of all the soldiers lodging with me, two or three only were wounded, and in these cases the wounds were slight and already beginning to heal." This was clearly untrue.

Edith Cavell was to spend ten weeks in the prison at St Gilles. Ironically enough it was not far from the new hospital staffed by her nurses which she had helped set up. She wrote to the clinic about money matters and asked Sister Wilkins to send her "some blue and white combs from my drawer, a little notebook and some hanks – also my *Imitation of Christ* – a little red book on my shelves – and my prayer book."

Her cell was sparsely furnished. It contained a table, which unfolded to make a bed, a chair, a small cupboard and a washbasin. Her nurses sent her flowers. She spent her time embroidering and reading her copy of *The*

Imitation of Christ over and over again. After so many years of bustling activity, she saw her solitude as a luxury. Later she was to tell the Reverend Stirling Gahan: "Life for me has always been hurried and full of difficulty. These weeks in prison have been a time of rest. I have had time to read, to pray and to reflect."

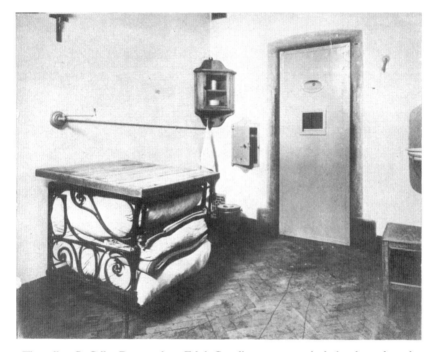

The cell in St Gilles Prison where Edith Cavell spent ten weeks before being brought to trial. "These weeks in prison have been a time of rest", she wrote. "I have had time to read, to pray, to reflect".

The Trial

Nine weeks after her arrest on 5th August she and her companions in the escape network were brought before a military tribunal for trial on 7th October. She was determined to face trial in civilian clothes, not in the Matron's uniform she had worn when she was arrested. She wrote: "Will you please send me at once: My blue coat and skirt, white muslin blouse, thick grey reindeer gloves, grey fur stole."

The charge against her was of "conducting soldiers to the enemy". When questioned about this she replied robustly: "My preoccupation has not been to aid the enemy but to help the men who applied to me to reach the frontier. Once across the frontier they were free." The trial of all the thirty five accused took just two days. There was no question of Edith Cavell being found 'Not Guilty'. She admitted what she had done. The only question was the severity of the sentence the tribunal would impose.

Determined not to bring her profession into disrepute, Edith Cavell dressed in civilian clothes for her trial.

The decision was in the hands of the Military Governor of Brussels – General von Sauberzweig. He was a bullet-headed Prussian cavalry officer who had instigated a reign of terror in Belgium. He was bitter because his son had been blinded fighting the British. This was to prove the opportunity for him to take his revenge.

The trial ended on Friday afternoon and sentence was not passed until the following Monday. By this time diplomatic moves were being made to ask for clemency. Brand Whitlock, the American Ambassador in Brussels, had earlier already written twice to the head of the German Political Office about Edith Cavell's arrest, but had had no reply. At this critical moment he was taken ill, and his deputy, 30 year-old Hugh Gibson, had to step into the breach.

Rumours had abounded over that weekend. Since Spain, as well as America, was a neutral in the war, Gibson enlisted the help of the experienced Spanish Ambassador, the Marquis de Villalober, to find out what was happening. Both of them called at the German Political Office and telephoned repeatedly to find out when sentence was being passed on Edith Cavell, and what it would be. Their questions were never answered. They were simply given the assurance that they would be told in due course. Then, on the Monday evening, the rumours became more persistent: Edith Cavell had been sentenced to death. She was to be shot at dawn next day.

Although by then it was late evening – 8.30pm – Gibson and Villalobar went at once to the Political Office. Here they were told that the official responsible, Baron von der Lancken, was at the theatre and was not expected back until midnight. Gibson insisted he was sent for. Arrived from the theatre, Baron von der Lancken proved charming. An experienced diplomat, he cast doubt on the rumours and suggested a meeting next morning. Hugh Gibson stood his ground. If the rumour were true, tomorrow would be too late. He insisted the Baron should telephone the presiding judge of the court martial to find out the truth.

The call was made. Unable to conceal matters any longer, the Baron confirmed that Edith Cavell was to be shot at dawn. Gibson then produced a formal Note from the American Ambassador appealing for clemency. Again the Baron played for time. He himself was powerless. The only person who could delay the death penalty was the Military Governor, General von Sauberzweig. Once more Gibson stood firm. Late though it was, the General must be telephoned.

Called to the telephone, the General proved inflexible. The Baron relayed his decision to the diplomats: 'He had acted in the case only after mature consideration. The sentence was that prescribed under paragraph 58 of the German Military Code. The offences were of such a character that he considered the immediate infliction of the death penalty is imperative. He therefore declined to accept the plea for clemency or any other representation in the matter. The Ambassador's Note would not be accepted.' There was nothing more that Gibson could do. It was now past midnight. Edith Cavell had seven hours to live.

Edith's Final Hours

The news she was to face the firing squad was brought to Edith Cavell at 8.30 that night by the German Army chaplain, Pastor le Seur. She blushed. "I understand," she replied. "How much time will they give me?" "Only, I fear, until tomorrow morning," he answered. "So little time," she said.

The Pastor did what little was within his power to help her. He told her he would try to arrange for the English chaplain, her friend the Reverend Stirling Gahan, to be allowed to bring her Communion in prison that evening. And he promised to come to the prison at dawn next day, travel with her to the firing range, and stay to the end. Then he set off to find Stirling Gahan.

After he left, Edith Cavell wrote a last letter to her nurses: "My dear nurses, It is a very sad moment when I write to say good bye to you all. The beautiful flowers you sent me have brought life and colour to my cell. The roses are still fresh but the chrysanthemums did not like prison life any more than I do – so they did not live very long. Everywhere in life we learn something new and if you were now in my place you would soon realise how precious is liberty and how grateful we should be to have it. I hope you will continue with your studies, just as though I were there, because in a short time you will have to undergo an examination, and I would like to have you ready for it. One last word – if there is one of you that has a grievance against me, I ask you to forgive me. Perhaps sometimes I have been too severe, but never voluntarily unjust, and I have loved you all much more than you thought. Truly yours, Edith Cavell."

Reverend Stirling Gahan,
the English Chaplain in Brussels

Stirling Gahan had been out much of the day trying to get news of Edith Cavell. When he finally reached home he found a pencilled note from Pastor le Seur waiting for him: "An English lady, who has not long to live, wishes to see you, and to receive Holy Communion." He went at once to the Pastor's house and was told the news. The Pastor handed him the permit allowing him to visit Edith Cavell in prison. He went back to fetch his Communion Set and hurried to the prison.

By the time he arrived it was almost 10pm and Edith Cavell had given up hope of seeing him. She had unfolded her bed ready for the night, and was in her dressing gown. As he entered she held out her hand. "How good of you to come," she said. They talked for a while. She was calm and composed. Her trial had been fairly conducted, and her sentence what she expected. "I have no fear or shrinking. I have seen death so often that it is not strange or fearful to me. This time of rest has been a great mercy. Everyone here has been very kind," she said. "This I would say, standing as I do in view of God and eternity, I realise that patriotism is not enough. I must have no hatred or bitterness towards anyone."

There was no table in the cell. They sat side by side on the bed with the one chair between them as their Communion table. They took the bread and wine. Stirling Gahan said the Blessing. Then together they spoke the words of Abide With Me.

> Abide with me; fast falls the eventide,
> The darkness deepens, Lord, with me abide.
> When other helpers fail, and comforts flee,
> Help of the helpless, O abide with me.
>
> I fear no foe with thee at hand to bless;
> Ills have no weight, and tears no bitterness.
> Where is death's sting? Where, grave, thy victory?
> I triumph still, if thou abide with me.
>
> Hold thou thy Cross before my closing eyes;
> Shine through the gloom, and point me to the skies:
> Heaven's morning breaks, and earth's vain shadows flee;
> In life, in death, O Lord, abide with me.

As Stirling Gahan turned to leave he said: "We shall always remember you as a heroine and a martyr." "Don't think of me like that," Edith Cavell replied. "Think of me only as a nurse who tried to do her duty." Next morning Pastor le Seur came for her. Modest to the last, she had pinned her skirt closely round her ankles to make sure she would be decently covered when she fell. Under armed escort they travelled together to the firing range. As they walked along the corridor she asked permission to complete her diary. She wrote: "Died at 7am October 12th 1915."

At the scene of the execution, the sentences were read aloud. The Pastor said the Grace quietly in English and led her to the execution post. She was bound to it and her eyes were bandaged. The Pastor saw they were filled with tears. There was a pause, which seemed like an eternity, while the priest finished speaking with Philippe Baucq, the architect who was to be executed with her. Then he, too, was led into position. A command rang out, two parties of eight men fired from a distance of six paces. Edith Cavell and Philippe Baucq were killed instantly.

Graves in St Gilles Prison.
Executed prisoners were buried at the prison in graves marked with a plain wooden cross. The shaft of the cross from Edith Cavell's grave is still kept at Swardeston Church.

General von Sauberzweig had reckoned, when he hurried through the execution of Edith Cavell that, once the deed was done, that would be the last anyone would hear of it. He miscalculated. Hugh Gibson and his colleagues lost no time in seeing that the full story came out. The press seized on it. The volley of shots fired on that October morning echoed round the world. In England *The Times* wrote: "The ordinary German mind is doubtless incapable of understanding the horror and disgust which the military execution of Miss Cavell will arouse throughout the civilised world. The chief business of Baron von der Lancken and of his staff appears to have been to mislead the American Minister until their military accomplices could put her to death without embarrassing intervention. We do not know whether the hide-bound brutality of the military authorities or the lying trickery of the civilians is more repulsive. Both were determined that Miss Cavell should die, and they conspired together to shoot her before an appeal could be lodged. They have killed an English Nurse, and by killing her they have immediately deepened the stain of infamy that degrades them in the eyes of the whole world. They could have done no deed better calculated to serve the British cause." And so it proved.

Remember Edith Cavell

The London Evening News front page. Newspapers throughout the world were outraged by the news of Edith Cavell's death.

The World Reads . . .

The sense of outrage at Edith Cavell's execution spread far beyond
Britain. France, Britain's ally in the war, was quick to react. *The
Intransigent* wrote:

"Is it not a condemnation of her butchers that they did not understand the
disgust that the murder would arouse?...The German who in cold blood,
without the excuse even of the heat of battle, condemns and executes Miss
Cavell is a monster, who has placed himself without the laws of man.
Today and tomorrow every Frenchman will know that the Germans have
destroyed a patron saint. The French soldiery will respond to that
knowledge with an enthusiasm that will overcome all fatigue, and the
crime of Miss Cavell's murder will weigh heavy in the scales in which the
fortunes of the Germans are now being tried."

The theme was taken up by the *Journal des Debats:*

"The assassination of Miss Cavell deserves to be avenged, and will be in
a fashion more terrible than the Germans can conceive... The souls of
England and France are united today before the body of poor noble Miss
Cavell in a solemn covenant."

France was already at war with Germany but in Holland – a neutral in
the war – *The New Rotterdam Courier* reaction was just as strong:

"One can only be astounded that a court consisting of men, who very
probably in similar circumstances would have done the same thing as Miss
Cavell, should have looked upon it as their duty to judge so hardly of a
woman. Still more astounding is it that the punishment should have been
carried out. This event is one of the most repulsive of any that have
occurred in this repulsive war. We consider it a lack of intelligence on the
part of Miss Cavell's judges if they believe that the sentence would serve
as a warning to others... On the contrary, the incident will aggravate the
feelings of bitter anger not only among Germany's enemies, but also in
neutral countries."

Rumours abounded that the firing squad refused to shoot Edith Cavell. This best-selling postcard shows Edith Cavell being shot with a revolver by a villainous German officer.

The most powerful neutral country was, of course, America, and the response in America was to prove a turning point in the war:

"In the story of the trial, sentence, plea for mercy and execution of Miss Cavell. there is lacking no circumstance that might be calculated to arouse the indignation and scorn of mankind." *The New York Evening Post*

"It seems as if a different moral language were spoken in Berlin than elsewhere. Official Germany is unable to understand why it is criticised, and the more official Germany defends itself the more it furnishes grounds for condemnation. Evidently it is still in a moral vacuum through which no sound of protest can penetrate – it is still in the grip of the same evil reasoning that brought on the war and is under the control of a fantasy that deprives it of the power to see things as they are." *The Globe*

"An atrocious exhibition of the barbarism of German military law and of the savagery of the German military character." *The Boston Transcript*

"What everybody who is not a German knows is that the Germans would have better lost an army corps than to have shot this woman for the comparatively trivial offence she committed. Her blood will blot the honour of the German Army and the German Government for generations to come… Centuries hence German historians will be apologising for the ruthlessness of the military commander who was unable to see *common sense* is mightier than the letter of military law." *The United States World*

"Execration unspeakable and horror inexpressible is the universal feeling in this country touching the murder of Miss Cavell." *Louisville Courier*

Even the German language newspaper in America could not withhold criticism:

"There are times when German commanders may do things in the heat of war in which their own people will not support them." *New York Staats Zeitung*

An angel bends to lay a laurel wreath on Edith's brow – one of many images that public imagination projected on Edith Cavell after her death.

Appalled by world reaction, the German propaganda machine belatedly tried to turn the tide of world opinion. One of the most damaging accusations was that they had promised to let the Americans know when sentence was passed and failed to do so. Relying on the letter of the law, they woodenly replied:

"Such a promise was never given by the German authorities... We must point out that the talk was between an employee of the Legation and a subordinate German officer so was not strictly of a diplomatic character." They then tried to show Edith Cavell as a money-grabber:

"With regard to the assertion that Miss Cavell unselfishly tended other persons, it must be pointed out that she earned her living by nursing and charging fees which only rich people were able to afford."

But it was the fact that Edith Cavell was a woman that aroused the indignation of the world. Desperately the German spin doctors tried to justify their action. *The Cologne Times* wrote:

"The person executed was a woman – that is after all the chief argument used against us by Englishmen and Americans. But if it had been a German woman who had been justly executed by the British, nobody in Germany would have blown it up into a moral issue. This is because the English and the Germans have totally different perceptions both about justice and about the status of women. We still remember the extremely mild judgement passed on Suffragettes in England just out of consideration for their sex. Women who only wanted to attract attention and often committed crimes out of perverse vanity were punished so mildly that, instead of having a frightening effect, it seemed to give encouragement to commit similar offences.

This could never be understood in Germany: We did not see any chivalry in the attitude of the English Authority, but an inferior kind of genuine justice – and a gross *injustice* against people who had to suffer from the stupid vandalism of crazy women.

The very people who sympathised with the women's cause had every reason to object to this untimely soft-heartedness, for this meant nothing else but: 'You women are intellectually and morally inferior, you cannot be taken seriously, and consequently you cannot be judged by the same principle as men!'

Miss Cavell has certainly proved herself to possess the power of mind and decision of a man: consequently it is only just that she should not be punished differently from a man. Are we to answer our brave and much-suffering soldiers in the trenches, whose opponents are being increased by the illegal manipulations of a woman: 'we cannot pass a normal sentence because it is a woman who has smuggled fighters into the lines of the enemy'?"

They were hopelessly out of their depth. The tide of passion released by Edith Cavell's death could not be held by back by words. In England during the next weeks the number of men volunteering for the Army doubled, and it was the sense of outrage at her death, perhaps more than anything else, that helped bring America into the war.

The English propagandists made the most of the opportunity that had been handed to them. When Edith Cavell was shot, she was fifty years old, and she was wearing civilian clothes. But postcards and posters of her death show a flowing-haired young girl, lying dead in her nurse's uniform. They became best sellers. In some, a helmeted German officer with a revolver stands above her. In one, an angel hovers over her in a shaft of light. The rumour sprang up that the firing squad had refused to obey orders and that their officer had drawn his revolver and shot her through the heart. The word "vengeance" was on everybody's lips.

Edith Cavell was buried near the rifle range in a grave marked by a wooden cross. After the war her body was brought back to England. Throughout the journey from Brussels to Dover it was escorted in turn by soldiers, by naval ratings and by nurses. As the train took the coffin to London, the railway stations it passed through were crowded with people come to pay their respects, and men stood bare-headed in the fields as the

Edith's coffin arrives at Thorpe Station, Norwich, for a mounted escort to Norwich Cathedral.

Edith's coffin is carried into Norwich Cathedral by men of the Norfolk Regiments. Among them was Sgt. Jesse Tunmore, one of the men she had sheltered.

train went by. In London there was a service in Westminster Abbey. Then once more crowds stood beside the railway line to salute the train as it made its way to Norwich Station where a gun carriage was waiting. Then to Norwich Cathedral, where one of the soldiers proud to carry her coffin was Sergeant Tunmore, whom she had hidden in the clinic. She was buried beside the Cathedral walls.

"Patriotism is not enough," said Edith Cavell in the last hours of her life, "I must have no hatred or bitterness towards anyone." It is a tragic irony that her death provoked an upsurge in hatred and bitterness, and cries for vengeance rang throughout the world.

As Edith Cavell discovered, forgiveness is at the heart of the Christian message. Vengeance solves nothing. This is the truth she came to understand in her prison cell. It is a lesson we still need to learn.

Edith Cavell's grave at 'Life's Green' outside Norwich Cathedral.

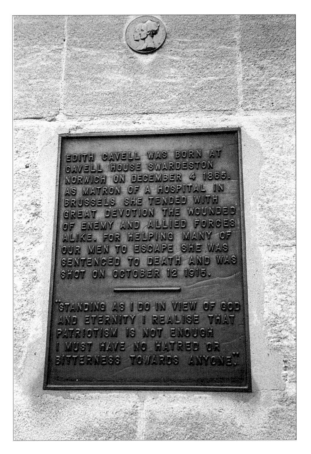

THE WORDS ON EDITH CAVELL'S STATUE WHICH STANDS BESIDE THE ERPINGHAM GATE TO NORWICH CATHEDRAL

Edith Cavell was born at Cavell House Swardeston Norwich on December 4 1865. As matron of a hospital in Brussels she tended with great devotion the wounded of enemy and allied forces alike. For helping many of our men to escape she was sentenced to death and was shot on October 12 1915.

"Standing as I do in view of God and eternity I realise that patriotism is not enough. I must have no hatred or bitterness towards anyone".

Recommendations for further reading

Considering the close association of the Cathedral with Edith Cavell, there are relatively few publications about her in the Dean & Chapter library. One might have expected there to be more.

However, what is there is of some interest. In addition to the books dealing with her life story, which you would expect to find, you will also find an account of lesser known items such as the Cavell memorabilia held in St. Mary & St. George church, Alberta, Canada. There is also the story of Mount Edith Cavell in Canada. I, for one, was surprised to learn that a mountain had been named after the Norfolk heroine.

Interest has always been strong in her trial and execution. The library has quite a lot of material on this. The most useful is contained in a volume entitled "The File". This contains typescripts of all the contemporary reports and documents from official and newspaper sources, recording the lead-up to, and world reaction to the events. This volume gives no indication of the author, but the typescripts have been bound up into a single volume. It contains information which might be difficult to track down elsewhere. There is also a very similar published work, by A. Got. This is based on previously unpublished documents, and although published in the 1940s, has only recently been given to the library.

Various Orders of Service are held, including a souvenir of the memorial service at Westminster Abbey in 1919 when her body was brought back to England en route to Norwich, and also the Order of Ceremony at Norwich Cathedral for the interment.

Some newspapers are held with the original reports of her execution in 1915 and others with the story of her return for burial in 1919. Some are originals, others are photocopies.

For me, the most poignant of the books are two that tell us nothing of her life or her story. These are two books that were her own; prizes won and which she must have treasured. Inside one of them are still the leaves and pressed flowers that perhaps she placed there herself.

Tom Mollard A.L.A.
Librarian, Dean & Chapter Library, Norwich Cathedral.

NORWICH CATHEDRAL
DEAN & CHAPTER LIBRARY

A list of books and other items in the library stock dealing with

EDITH CAVELL

BOSTON, Noel. The dutiful Edith Cavell. n.d. shelf E8

CLARKE-KENNEDY. Edith Cavell, Pioneer and patriot. 1965 shelf E.8

DAUNTON, Claire ed. Edith Cavell, her life and her art. Royal London Hospital. c 1990. shelf E2

EDITH CAVELL: Memorabilia in St. Mary & St. George church, Alberta. Canada. Text and photographs. (In ring binder) shelf K.4

EDITH CAVELL: 1865-1915. 'A Norfolk heroine' Swardeston PCC. 1982

FELSTEAD, S. T. Edith Cavell; the crime that shook the world. Written from the dossier of the former German secret police and the personal narratives of survivors. n.d. shelf K.5

THE FILE: documents relating to the trial of Edith Cavell. [transcripts] shelf E2

GOT, A. The case of Miss Cavell, from the unpublished documents of the trial; the property of a former commissary of the German government. 1946 shelf K.8

GRANT, Sally. Edith Cavell. 1865-1915.. Larks Press 1995 shelf E3

HOEHLING, A. A. Edith Cavell. Cassell 1958. E8

JOHNS, R. Nurse Cavell. dog lover. 1934 Shelf E.8

PITCHER, John. Mount Edith Cavell; in the heart of the sub-alpine. Canada. 1982 Shelf E.2

TEMERSON, H. Edith Cavell. 1865-1915 1965 shelf E.8

RELIGIOUS SERVICES

1 – Order of ceremony – 15th. May 1919. (9pp.)

2 – Jubilee Memorial Service: 12th. October 1965. (7pp.)

3 – Evensong, Swardeston Parish Church. 4th. December 1965. [marking centenary of her birth]
all pasted into the back of
"Edith Cavell, pioneer and patriot" by A. E. Clark-Kennedy

4 – "In Memoriam" – Souvenir of the memorial service at Westminster Abbey. May 15th. 1919.

5 – Re-dedication; order of service. Tombland 4th. December 1992

ASSOCIATIONS WITH

Edith Cavell Secondary School, Enfield Rd. London. Cavellian Scroll Souvenir Edition. October 1965 [School magazine]. shelf E.8

Thomas à Kempis. Imitation of Christ. [facsimile of her copy] shelf E.8

Sacred Gleanings – safe

Holy Bible – safe (2 vols. awarded as school prizes to Edith Cavell)

NEWSPAPERS

[London] Evening News October 22nd. 1915

Daily Mirror. September 5th. 1919 (Photocopy)

Daily Mirror. May 16th. 1919

Daily Sketch. May 16th. 1919

EPHEMERA

Misc. assorted photographs, postcards, bookmark etc

Other Norwich Cathedral Publications

This book is just one of a series of books published by Norwich Cathedral Publications which hopes to make a Christian interpretation of some of the many resources, treasures and historic subjects associated with this remarkable building. I hope your enjoyment of this book enthuses you to read some more in this series. Details of what we have to offer are listed below and new titles are in preparation.

Phillip McFadyen, General Editor.
Norwich Cathedral Publications Ltd.

The Organs of Norwich Cathedral
Simon Burrell & Mark Nicholas

A brief history of the various organs during the lifetime of the cathedral together with technical specifications of the main organ, the Snetzler Chamber Organ and the Coffin Chamber Organ. Listed are the known organists of Norwich Cathedral since 1333.
(6 colour pictures, 1 b/w).

ISBN 0 9535493 0 5

An Eye on Heaven
The Biblical Bosses of Norwich Cathedral
Phillip McFadyen

By craning your neck or using mirrors the bosses in the nave roof can just be seen. This book contains 34 wonderful full colour drawings by the author of the bosses which present the stories from the Creation to Solomon. These drawings are accompanied by an interpretation of the stories carved in stone by these 15th century craftsmen.

ISBN 0 9535493 1 3

The Black Monks' Workshop
An Introduction to Norwich Cathedral Cloister & Priory
John Nicholls

This book is for people who have been looking around the Cathedral and wish to explore the history of this wonderful building further. In two sections it initially provides a concise yet vivid history of the priory together with a plan. The future plans for the Cathedral are also described. The second section is based on a 'guided' walk through the Cloisters and depicts all of the bosses in this part of the cathedral.
(7 colour pictures, 7 other b/w drawings).

ISBN 0 9535493 2 1